Workshops
That
Really
Work

Workshops
That
Really
Work

The ABC's of
Designing and Delivering
Sensational Presentations

Hal Portner

CORWIN PRESS
A SAGE Publications Company
Thousand Oaks, California

For information:

Corwin Press
A Sage Publications Company
2455 Teller Road
Thousand Oaks, California 91320
www.corwinpress.com

Sage Publications Ltd.
1 Oliver's Yard
55 City Road
London EC1Y 1SP
United Kingdom

Sage Publications India Pvt. Ltd.
B-42, Panchsheel Enclave
Post Box 4109
New Delhi 110 017 India

Printed in the United States of America

Library of Congress Cataloging-in-Publication Data

Portner, Hal.
Workshops that really work: The ABC's of designing and delivering sensational presentations / Hal Portner.
    p. cm.
Includes bibliographical references and index.
ISBN 1–4129–1511–2 (cloth)—ISBN 1–4129–1512–0 (pbk.)
    1. Teachers' workshops—Planning. 2. Educational consultants. I. Title.
LB1743.P67 2006
370.'71'55—dc22   2005015256

This book is printed on acid-free paper.

05   06   07   08   09   10   9   8   7   6   5   4   3   2   1

Acquisitions Editor:	Rachel Livsey
Editorial Assistant:	Phyllis Cappello
Production Editor:	Beth A. Bernstein
Copy Editor:	Jacqueline A. Tasch
Typesetter:	C&M Digitals (P) Ltd.
Proofreader:	Dennis Webb
Indexer:	Rick Hurd
Cover Designer:	Rose Storey

Contents

Introduction

I t is the nature of educators to want to help others learn. Teachers express this desire by instructing and guiding students; administrators by leading and enabling teachers. Some teachers and administrators assuage their desire to help others grow by mentoring and peer-coaching colleagues. Gabriel Díaz-Maggioli (2004) echoes my own feelings about educators sharing their expertise with colleagues when he writes

> My vision of professional development is grounded in faith in [educators and] the institutions they work for. . . . Effective professional development should be understood as a . . . commitment that [educators] make in order to further the purposes of the profession while addressing their own particular needs. It should follow the principles that guide the learning practices of experienced adults, in teaching communities that foster cooperation and shared expertise. [Educator] success stories are living theories of educational quality and should be shared with the wider educational community for the benefit of all involved. (p. 3)

Most of us know veteran teachers and administrators—some retired, others still in full-time positions—who lead workshops, offer sessions at conferences, or otherwise share their expertise in formal presentations. We also know of others who have never presented a workshop for colleagues and would like to do so. I have had several conversations with colleagues and read Internet postings by educators who will be presenting workshops or conference sessions for the first time. Quite a few of these veteran teachers and administrators look on the opportunity with a mixture of anticipation and trepidation. Many of us recall how, as first-year teachers, we suffered the excitement and uncertainties associated with taking on the first-time responsibilities of teaching. It comes as no surprise, then, that experienced teachers and administrators who for the first time assume the role of presenter undergo comparable feelings.

Usually, new presenters—and many veteran ones as well—are clear about the content they will present, and they generally assume they can trust their teaching experience to guide the process and keep their interactions with adult participants on the right track. However, I've found that quite a few presenters don't know what they don't know. That is to say, they don't realize the extent to which they will have to plan and prepare. They haven't thought through the particulars of selecting and introducing appropriate activities or considered under what circumstances to lecture or when best to rely on interactive strategies. They may be unaware of the potential value and pitfalls of visual aids such as handouts and PowerPoint presentations that are designed specifically for use with adults. Novice presenters usually do, however, sense that they would benefit from learning specific skills to guide their behaviors and from acquiring practical information to help them make better decisions. The purpose of this book is to help its readers develop those skills and apply those strategies.

ABOUT THIS BOOK

Let me introduce you to Kathy. Although Kathy is a fictional person, she represents the sort of veteran educator who has made the commitment to become a workshop presenter. We will follow Kathy as she progresses from novice to successful presenter. The book chronicles Kathy's journey and examines the strategies and resources she uses en route.

My role in Kathy's development as a presenter—and hopefully in yours, the reader—is that of mentor. As such, I provide opportunities to reflect on actions and decisions, offer strategies and resources, and guide the acquisition and application of relevant knowledge, understandings, and skills.

Chapter 1 follows Kathy as she goes through the introspective process of deciding whether she is both willing and able to become a presenter. It then offers the reader a structured opportunity to do the same.

Chapter 2 enlightens Kathy on the critical differences between teaching children and teaching adults and heightens her awareness of learning style preferences. It goes on to examine the advantages of applying these understandings to the development and presentation of a workshop for adults.

Chapter 3 helps Kathy design a presentation. It guides her through a series of steps and provides you, the reader, with the opportunity to use the same structured organizer to design your own workshop presentation.

Chapter 4 provides Kathy with a set of good presenting principles and helps her effectively apply them in her workshop.

Chapter 5 touches on many of the issues Kathy might face and strategies she might use should she decide to expand her opportunities and market herself as a presenter.

A resource section contains instruments, samples, and references to support and enhance the discussions in the chapters.

DEFINITIONS AND CLARIFICATIONS

It will be helpful for the reader to understand how I use several words and terms throughout this book.

Presenting a workshop is a form of teaching in which you invite those in attendance (*participants*) to interact with you and each other in the exploration of a professional issue, curriculum content, or instructional methodology.

Presenting information refers to such activities as giving a keynote address or describing a model program to a group of colleagues. It involves standing (or perhaps sitting) in front of (or perhaps in the middle of) an assemblage of people (*attendees*) for the purpose of informing, inspiring, and/or persuading.

Facilitating plays an important role in the presenting process. Facilitating means providing the structure and guiding the process to enable participants to make and carry out their own informed decisions.

Staff developers, especially those who lead professional development sessions in their own school or district, may well find themselves providing *follow-up assistance;* that is to say, supporting the teacher's implementation of newly learned methods or materials in the days and weeks following the workshop itself.

PRESENTERS AS LEADERS AND LEARNERS

> Rather than putting theory into practice, we should put *ourselves* (sic) into practice by making a determined attempt to research our own practices and to find out the symbolic readings of our actions made by those with whom we work. Instead of selling ourselves as omniscient content and process experts, we should make [participants] aware of the resources that their own experiences represent. (Brookfield, 1993, pp. 11–12)

Presenting workshops and providing follow-up assistance offer many ancillary benefits for veteran teachers. Presenters say that they gain as much as they give in terms of their own professional development, improvement of their own practice, and deeply felt satisfaction from being a contributing member to the profession. Presenting also provides an opportunity for experienced teachers to see their profession from a new perspective. While preparing presentations, they often gain insight into their own practice as well as learning from the practices of those around them.

Acknowledgments

It was Tom Ganser, director of the Office of Field Experiences at University of Wisconsin-Whitewater and an associate professor in the Department of Curriculum and Instruction, who planted the idea for this book in my subconscious. As you can see, the idea has taken root. Thank you, Tom.

The person whose brain I pick when I need suggestions and feedback is my friend and colleague, Robert Pauker. Dr. Pauker, who lives in Glastonbury, Connecticut, is an outstanding consultant and presenter whose counsel I value greatly. Thank you, Bob.

I also owe a great deal of gratitude to the thousands of people who have attended my presentations over the years. I hope they benefited from their participation; I certainly have learned much about presenting as a result of working with them. Thank you all.

The contributions of the following reviewers are gratefully acknowledged:

Kendall Zoller
Independent Educational Consultant
Auburn, CA

Arthur Beachamp
Director
Sacramento Area Science Project
University of California, Davis
Davis, CA

Suzanne L. Gilmour, PhD
Chair
Educational Administration Department
Executive Director

New York State Association for Women in Administration
State University of New York, Oswego
Oswego, NY

Joellen Killion
Director of Special Projects
National Staff Development Council
Arvada, CO

Mark Bower
Director of Staff Development
Technology and Continuing Education
Hilton Central School District
Hilton, NY

About the Author

 **Hal Portner** regularly presents to and consults with school districts and other educational organizations and institutions. He writes, develops materials, trains mentors, and facilitates the development of new-teacher induction programs. Hal is a former public school teacher and administrator and was a staff consultant for the Connecticut State Department of Education where, among other responsibilities, he served as Coordinator of the Connecticut Institute for Teaching and Learning and worked closely with school districts to develop and carry out professional development and teacher evaluation plans and programs. He also served as professional development consultant for the faculty of Holyoke (Massachusetts) Community College. Mr. Portner is a member of the Editorial Board of *Mentoring & Tutoring*, a peer-reviewed international journal. He is the author of *Mentoring New Teachers* (1998, 2003), *Training Mentors Is Not Enough: Everything Else Schools and Districts Need to Do* (2001), and *Being Mentored: A Guide for Protégés* (2002); he is the editor of *Teacher Mentoring and Induction: The State of the Art and Beyond*, all published by Corwin Press.

Chapter One

Assessing Your Potential as a Presenter

Try as she might, Kathy couldn't keep the corners of her mouth from turning up into a faint smile as she walked into the teacher's room Friday afternoon. "Why the grin, Kath," asked Justin, "just win the lottery?"

Kathy's smile broadened. Justin, who taught in the classroom next to hers, smiled back. "I just left Georgette's office," she replied. "She told me how impressed she was by how effectively I use a new instructional methodology in my classroom and how much the students have improved since I started using it."

"Way to go, Kath! Georgette always struck me as the kind of principal who recognizes the good things that teachers do in the classroom."

"But that's not all." Kathy's sparkling eyes made her smile even brighter. "Georgette invited me to share the methodology with other teachers in the school. She asked me to consider presenting a workshop on the topic at our school's Professional Development Day next month."

Justin raised his arm and gave Kathy a high-five. "Wow, that's great," he said. "Are you going to do it? I know you'd do a great job."

"Yeah, well . . ." Kathy's smile faded a bit, and her eyes lowered. "Between you and me, Justin, I'm not so sure. Yes, I know I am a good teacher, and I know the methodology backwards and forwards, but standing there in front of teachers I work with every day . . . I don't know that I've got the courage, or for that matter the temperament to do it. Georgette asked me to think about it over the weekend and let her know on Monday."

PREDISPOSITION

Why would any teacher seek to take on the added task of presenting a workshop to fellow teachers? Although not every teacher desires to work with adult colleagues, many educators do choose to extend their commitment to teaching and to the profession by assuming additional roles that extend their own learning and allow them to share what they know with others (Steffy, Wolfe, Pasch, & Enz, 2000). Educators with the predisposition to share professional knowledge and expertise with colleagues are open-minded and flexible, have the desire to assist and nurture others, seek opportunities to learn and improve, and possess effective interpersonal skills.

Does Kathy possess such a predisposition? She is an excellent teacher, and excellent teachers continually look for ways to challenge themselves professionally. For Kathy, would taking on the role of presenter be a way to meet that challenge? Let's help her decide by asking her to reflect on some open-ended questions.

- Kathy, what examples can you cite that make you feel that you know enough about the methodology to be able to present it effectively to others?

Kathy's reflection: I first learned about the methodology from an article in a professional journal and then participated in a workshop presented by the person who developed it. When I first tried out the methodology in the classroom, it was only moderately successfully, so I e-mailed the presenter with specific questions and received some specific and very helpful suggestions. I kept assessing and modifying until the strategies became quite effective as evidenced by significant improvement in student test results.

- Your workshop participants will want to come away with strategies on how to use the methodology effectively in the classroom. What makes you think you would feel comfortable sharing your strategies with your fellow teachers?

Kathy's reflection: I'm really not sure I would be that comfortable. I'm concerned that my colleagues might think me a pretentious know-it-all showoff. However, I truly believe in the value of the methodology and think others would find it useful. Perhaps if I had more confidence in being able to present a workshop . . .

- What characteristics do you have that lead you to believe that your presentation would be interesting and useful to participants?

Kathy's reflection: I'm a good teacher so I should be able to teach other teachers and keep them enthused while doing so. I think that I understand how to vary my teaching methods to account for various types of learners and that I am flexible enough to adjust and modify along the way. I am a bit concerned, however, that I may tend to treat adults as children when I am teaching them . . . for example, I would have to be careful that I didn't get too "cutesy" or simplistic and say things like, "Quiet down when I place my hand on my head."

- What responsibilities, personal as well as professional, do you have that might be affected if you took on this additional obligation?

Kathy's reflection: It would probably make additional demands on my already full schedule and perhaps cut into the time I would normally devote to other responsibilities, such as preparing for my regular classes. But then again, I might find myself energized by the experience. As for my family and friends, if I end up enjoying making presentations, I know they will support me, and I, in turn, might even end up being a more interesting person to be with.

- What do you expect to gain personally and professionally as a result of presenting the workshop?

Kathy's reflection: I suspect that successfully presenting a workshop would increase my self-esteem, making me feel as though I have contributed to the profession in general and specifically to the effectiveness of other teachers. I also think that my own use of the new instructional methodology will improve because in order for me to effectively pass it on to others, I will need to be clear in my own head about how I apply it in the classroom. Also, I would be able to add "workshop presenter" to my résumé and perhaps become a "teacher leader" in my school.

We will learn Kathy's decision in the next chapter. Meanwhile, how about you? Do you have the courage, motivation, and temperament to present a workshop to your colleagues? Exercise 1.1 will help you assess your own predisposition.

Exercise 1.1   Do You Have the Motivation?

Directions: Fill in the blanks in the numbered order. Take time to think about the ramifications of your answers before writing them down. Feel free to discuss the questions with others.

1. If you were to present a workshop, the topic of the presentation would be

2. Why did you select this topic?

3. Why would anyone want to learn about this topic from you rather than from someone else?

4. Do you know enough about the presentation topic and how to apply it effectively to make what you would present useful to others? What are some examples that support your answer?

5. Do you have enough confidence in your ability to make your presentation interesting and useful to participants? What are some examples that support your answer?

6. What characteristics do you possess that would make you a good workshop presenter? What are some examples that support your answer?

7. It is possible that you may not know what you don't know about presenting a workshop and may need to ask for help. How comfortable would you be asking for help? Who might you ask, and why?

8. Will you be able to handle the time and responsibility associated with taking on the additional role? What previous experiences support your answer?

9. What can you expect to gain, personally and professionally, as a result of presenting the workshop?

10. Close your eyes and let your imagination take you into the future. Imagine you are in the middle of presenting a workshop to your fellow teachers. What is your body experiencing? What are your thoughts? How are the participants reacting?

11. In summary (check one), you want to _____ you do not want to _____ present a workshop because

PRESENTATION SKILLS AND BEHAVIORS

Having the courage, motivation, and temperament to present a workshop to your colleagues is critical, of course, but not the whole story. An effective presenter must

> *Exude confidence* by being familiar with the topic, having a comprehensive and workable presentation plan, and maintaining good physical and emotional health.
>
> *Encourage participation* by exhibiting such behaviors as letting individuals know that you noticed what they did or said and how it was helpful, asking individuals by name for their opinion, and recognizing the contributions of participants.
>
> *Be sensitive to participants' well-being* by being sure that the environment is physically and psychologically comfortable, avoiding long lectures, steering clear of periods of interminable sitting, and providing some form of refreshments.
>
> *Clarify expectations* by taking time early on to articulate your own objectives and allowing participants to express theirs.
>
> *Provide for dialogue* by employing small group discussion and by using open-ended questions to draw out participants' knowledge and experience.
>
> *Control pace and direction* by balancing the presentation of new material, discussion, and the clock.
>
> *Enhance understanding* by using resources geared to visual, auditory, and tactile learners.
>
> *Build on participants' knowledge* by finding out their experience ahead of time, acknowledging that experience during the session, and relating new learning to that experience.

These and other presenting skills and behaviors will be discussed in more detail in subsequent chapters, but meanwhile, Exercise 1.2 will help you assess the extent to which you already have these attributes. Because it may be tempting to write off the following exercise by simply rating yourself high on the items, I've asked you to reflect on your answers by citing specific examples—either positive or negative—from your own experience and then determining your level of confidence when it comes down to actually applying each one.

Exercise 1.2   Do You Have the Skills and Behaviors?

Directions: Think about the skill or behavior described in Column 1. In Column 2, describe a specific example where you used that skill or behavior, either successfully or not. In Column 3, indicate whether you feel V (very comfortable), M (moderately comfortable), or U (uncomfortable) using this skill or behavior.

Skill or Behavior	*Examples From My Experience*	*Confidence Level*
Exude confidence		
Encourage participation		
Be sensitive to participants' needs		
Have clear expectations		

(Continued)

Exercise 1.2   (Continued)

Skill or Behavior	Examples From My Experience	Confidence Level
Provide opportunity for dialogue		
Control pace and direction		
Enhance understanding		
Build on existing knowledge		

CHAPTER TWO

Understanding Adult Learners

Monday morning Kathy strode confidently into her principal's office. "If you still want me to, Georgette," she said," I would like to take you up on your suggestion that I lead a workshop at our next professional development day."

"Wonderful! Thanks for agreeing to do it, Kathy. I know several teachers who are curious about your new instructional methodology and how successfully you have applied it. They will be pleased to see your session on the list of workshops being offered."

"As you know, Georgette, I've never presented a workshop before. I know I'm a good teacher of children, but when it comes to adults . . ."

Georgette nodded. "Adults do have a different time perspective and set of experiences than children, which in turn produces a difference in the way adults approach learning."

"Where can I find out more about how adults learn?" asked Kathy.

"Talk with Drew. He heads up the town's adult education program and not only has a good grasp of the characteristics of adult learners, but also understands how to apply those characteristics in the adult classroom. Give Drew a call. I'm sure he will appreciate your interest in teaching adults and be happy to share his knowledge of the subject with you."

CHARACTERISTICS OF ADULT LEARNERS

Drew did indeed appreciate Kathy's interest in the characteristics of adult learning as well as her willingness to learn about the implications these characteristics might have on her workshop presentation. Kathy's entire teaching experience has involved only children. She listened carefully as Drew described how adults learn differently from children.

Drew explained to Kathy that the most obvious difference between adult and child learning styles is that adults have accumulated a foundation of *life experiences* and *knowledge* that includes work-related activities, family responsibilities, and previous education. Adults learn more readily when they can connect learning to their knowledge and experience. To help them do so, a workshop presenter should elicit participants' experience and knowledge and relate theories and concepts to their backgrounds. For example,

Drew suggested that Kathy should build into her workshop activities that encourage participants to share their experiences in relation to the topic being presented.

Adults are also *autonomous* and *self-directed,* Drew pointed out. They need to be free to direct themselves at times. A presenter must actively involve adult participants in the learning process. For example, give participants the opportunity to assume responsibility for presentations and group leadership. The presenter's role during this time is to act as facilitator, guiding participants to their own knowledge by asking open-ended questions and generally resisting the temptation to supply them with answers or other data except to inform their efforts.

Adults are *goal oriented* and *relevancy oriented.* They usually know what they want to attain, and it is the presenter's responsibility to find out what their goals are and to address those goals in the presentation. A relevancy orientation means that adults learn best when they see a reason for learning, so the workshop has to be applicable to their work or other responsibilities in order for it to be of value to them. Adults will appreciate a program that is organized and has clearly defined elements. The presenter must show participants early on that what they can expect to learn will help them attain their goals.

Drew reminded Kathy to keep in mind that adults are *practical.* They will focus on the aspects of the presentation most useful to them in their work. He emphasized that the presenter must show participants explicitly how their learning will be useful to them on the job.

Finally, Drew advised Kathy to remember that, like all learners, adults need to be shown *respect.* "You can do this," he suggested, "by acknowledging the wealth of experiences that adult participants bring to the workshop and providing the opportunity for them to voice their opinions freely."

Paying Attentions to Adult Characteristics

Drew shared with Kathy some suggestions he learned from Ron and Susan Zemke (1984), describing how adult learning characteristics influence the way workshops need to be planned and presented.

- The learning environment must be physically and psychologically comfortable; long lectures, periods of interminable sitting, and the absence of practice opportunities rate high on the irritation scale.
- Adults have something real to lose in a [workshop] situation. Self-esteem and ego are on the line when they are asked to risk trying a new behavior in front of peers and cohorts. Bad experiences in traditional education, feelings about authority, and the preoccupation with events outside the classroom affect in-class experience.
- Adults bring a great deal of life experience into the [workshop], an invaluable asset to be acknowledged, tapped, and used. Adults can learn well—and much—from dialogue with respected peers.
- Straightforward how-to is the preferred content. Adults cite a need for application and "how-to information" as their primary reason for participating in a workshop.
- [Presenters] who have a tendency to hold forth rather than facilitate can hold that tendency in check—or compensate for it—by concentrating on the use of open-ended questions to draw out relevant [participant] knowledge and experience.
- New knowledge has to be integrated with previous knowledge; [participants] must actively participate in the learning experience. The [participant] is dependent on the [presenter] for confirming feedback on skill practice; the [presenter] is dependent on the [participant] for feedback [on the relevancy and effectiveness of the presentation].
- The key to the [presenter] role is control. The [presenter] must balance the presentation of new material, debate and discussion, sharing of relevant experiences, and the clock. Ironically, it seems that [presenters] are best able to establish control when they risk giving it up. When they shelve egos and stifle the tendency to be threatened by challenge to plans and methods, they gain the kind of facilitative control needed to effect adult learning.
- The [presenter] has to protect minority opinion, keep disagreements civil and unheated, make connections between various opinions and ideas, and keep reminding the group

of the variety of potential solutions to the problem. The [presenter] is less advocate than orchestrator.

- Integration of new knowledge and skill requires transition time and focused effort on application.

Diverting Potential Resistance

Drew cautioned Kathy that these suggestions, while valuable, don't guarantee full participation from everyone. While some workshop participants will enter the experience with positive expectations, others may initially resist participating fully. Reasons for a negative attitude might include recalling past experiences that were perceived as a poor or irrelevant presentation, lacking interest in the topic, or having higher priorities as to how they use their professional time. The presenter will need to divert or overcome any initial resistance, preferably before it takes hold. One way to do this is by *framing* the activities.

Rich Allen (2005) describes framing this way:

People have certain perspectives, points of view, or *frames*, which exert a powerful influence on their perception of events. For example, imagine a minor car accident in which no one is injured. One driver may view it as a terrible event, since they have damaged their new car. Another driver may view it as a blessing, since they have emerged unscathed . . . Both had similar experiences, but their subsequent outlook and attitude are distinctly colored by the frame they choose to wrap around the circumstance. (p. 53)

Translated to a workshop setting, this means that each participant approaches an activity with a personal mental frame. Therefore, how people participate and what they get out of the workshop will differ from one individual to the next. Eller (2004) suggests that a presenter "will need to create a common frame that will help focus participants on the intended objective. In framing, the [presenter] draws a verbal boundary around the [activity]. The [presenter] also assumes some control over the group by setting the boundaries" (p. 61).

Kathy asked for an example of how to frame an activity. "At the start of an activity," Drew said, "take a moment to provide participants not only with some idea of what will be covered, but also with an explanation of why it is relevant to the topic of the session. Suppose that the workshop's topic is problem-based learning. The objective of one of the workshop's activities is to design problems for students working in groups that will induce the students to use critical thinking. You might frame the activity by handing participants an outline of Bloom's taxonomy and encouraging them to use to Bloom's cognitive levels as a guide for constructing their problems (Bloom, 2000)."

ADDRESS ADULT LEARNERS' EXPECTATIONS

You need to help participants understand how they will benefit from their participation. For example, how will participation in your workshop enhance their teaching and help their students learn better? If you know their expectations up front, you can periodically show them the relationship between those expectations and what they are learning.

Kathy wondered if she should ask her principal what she would like the teachers to learn and how she expects them to use what they learn. While Georgette's expectations are important, Drew pointed out that the advice of a school principal on "what teachers need" does not necessarily correspond to what the teachers themselves want to get out of participating. The answer may be somewhere in between. Therefore, it's important to find out what the participants themselves expect from the workshop.

In Kathy's case, because she's presenting a workshop to colleagues at her own school, she can just ask them. Faculty-room conversations would provide an excellent opportunity. Another approach is this: Early in the workshop—perhaps even before the session formally begins—ask participants to list their expectations on newsprint you've tacked up on a wall. Toward the end of the workshop, review the posted list. Check off the expectations and concerns that have been addressed, and deal briefly with any that have not.

ADULT LEARNING MODES

Another area of concern in developing workshop presentations is the different ways people take in and process information. As you probably know, there are visual, auditory, and tactile learners. Those of you who are teachers are used to these learning modes from working with children, and they apply to adults as well. You'll find they are helpful in planning and presenting workshops.

Visual learners learn best through seeing: These learners need to see the presenter's body language and facial expression. They tend to prefer sitting at the front of the room to avoid visual obstructions (e.g., people's heads). They may think in pictures and learn best from visual displays including diagrams, illustrations, overhead transparencies, videos, flipcharts, and handouts. During a lecture or discussion, visual learners often prefer to take detailed notes.

Auditory learners learn best through listening: They prefer verbal lectures and discussions, talking things through and listening to what others have to say. Auditory learners interpret the underlying meanings of speech through listening to tone of voice, pitch, speed, and other nuances. Written information may have little meaning *to them* until *they hear it.* These learners often benefit from reading text aloud and using a tape recorder.

Tactile/kinesthetic learners learn best through moving, doing, and touching: They prefer a hands-on approach, actively exploring the physical world around them. They may find it hard to sit still for long periods and may become distracted by their need for activity and exploration.

All three modes need to be used in the presentation, and the presenter needs to be sensitive to which mode various participants prefer. Most people access all three modes but tend to rely on one more than the others.

Determining Preferred Modes

To determine whether someone prefers visual, auditory, or tactile modes, ask workshop participants how they usually give directions when asked how to get to a particular location and how they prefer to receive such directions themselves. Do they like maps? Or do they prefer directions that name streets and specify left and right turns?

Also, depending on their preference, people tend to use sensory predicates such as *see, hear, feel, look,* and *listen* when they speak. For example, if a person were to say, "I don't see how doing what you suggest would work in my classroom," your response will be more effective by using the same mode in your reply (in this case, visual) by saying something like, "Look at it this way . . . " and following up by diagramming what you mean on newsprint.

Kathy likes to doodle while thinking or listening, which suggests that she's a visual person. Auditory learners might follow directions even though they may not appear to be listening, while those preferring a tactile/kinesthetic mode often fiddle with objects and punctuate their words with gestures.

Drew gave Kathy an inventory to check out her preferred learning mode (see Resource A: Dr. Richard L. Oliver's *Learning Style Inventory*). "It only takes a few minutes," he told Kathy. "In fact, your participants can complete it before the workshop and share their preferred modes with you and each other."

The results of Kathy's *Learning Style Inventory* verified that her preferred mode was visual . . . which probably explains why her notes on adult learning characteristics looked like those in Figure 2.1.

MULTIPLE INTELLIGENCES

Drew had one more aspect of adult learning to discuss with Kathy: multiple intelligences. Multiple intelligence theory was developed by Howard Gardner (1983). Gardner sees the human mind "as a series of relatively separate faculties, with only loose and non-predictable relations with one another, [rather] than a single all-purpose machine that performs steadily at a certain horsepower, independent of content and context" (Gardner, 1999, p. 32). So far, eight intelligences—eight qualitatively independent ways to be intelligent—have been identified. They are:

Verbal linguistic intelligence (sensitive to the meaning and order of words). Use activities that involve hearing, listening, impromptu or formal speaking, tongue twisters, humor, oral or silent reading, documentation, creative writing, spelling, journal, poetry.

Figure 2.1   Kathy's Notes

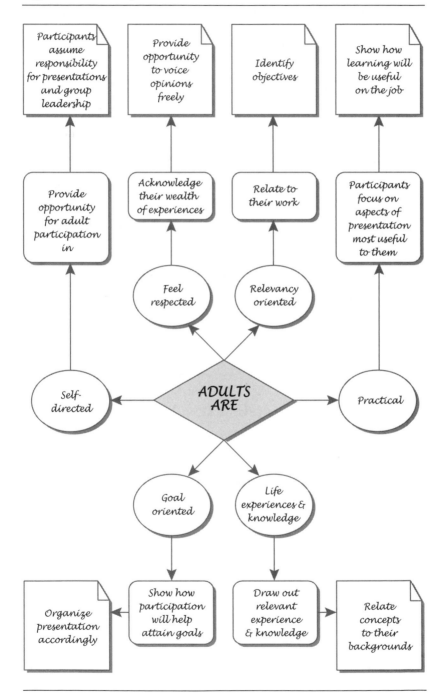

Logical-mathematical intelligence (able to handle chains of reasoning and recognize patterns and orders). Use activities that involve abstract symbols/formulas, outlining, graphic organizers, numeric sequences, calculation, deciphering codes, problem solving.

Musical intelligence (sensitive to pitch, melody, rhythm, and tone). Use activities that involve audiotape, music recitals, singing on key, whistling, humming, environmental sounds, percussion vibrations, rhythmic patterns, music composition, tonal patterns.

Spatial intelligence (able to perceive the world accurately and to re-create or transform aspects of that world). Use activities that involve art, pictures, sculpture, drawings, doodling, mind mapping, patterns/designs, color schemes, active imagination, imagery, block building.

Bodily Kinesthetic intelligence (able to use the body skillfully and handle objects adroitly). Use activities that involve role playing, physical gestures, drama, inventing, ball passing, sports games, physical exercise, body language, dancing.

Interpersonal intelligence (able to understand people and relationships). Use activities that involve group projects, division of labor, sensing others' motives, receiving/giving feedback, collaboration skills.

Intrapersonal intelligence (able to access one's emotional life as a means to understand oneself and others). Use activities that involve emotional processing, silent reflection methods, thinking strategies, concentration skills, higher order reasoning, "centering" practices, meta-cognitive techniques.

In the mid 1990s, under the auspices of the National Center for the Study of Adult Learning and Literacy at Harvard's Graduate School of Education, Viens and Kallenbach (2004) undertook the Adult Multiple Intelligences (AMI) Study in order to understand what the theory of multiple intelligences might have to offer to the field of adult teaching and learning.

The AMI Study validated what teachers of adults already knew when they used diverse classroom practices: Students participate more fully and more confidently when they have more control over how they process and demonstrate their learning. One interesting finding of the study was that when their more developed intelligences were allowed to come into play, the learning of some initially resistant learners became more individualized and increasingly under their control, and they became more involved.

After her conversation with Drew and additional encouragement from Georgette, Kathy felt ready to plan her presentation.

CHAPTER THREE

Designing the Presentation

K athy knows the importance of developing carefully thought-out and structured lesson plans for teaching students. Lesson plans help teachers organize content, materials, and methods. A well-designed plan not only assures student involvement and enhances student learning, but also helps the teacher feel more prepared and less stressed.

Kathy wants her workshop presentation to go well, so she decides to develop a lesson plan to guide her through her first experience teaching adults. Her typical student lesson plan contains learning objectives, instructional procedures, required materials, and some written description of how the students will be evaluated. However, rather than following her usual format in her usual way, Kathy decides to begin by applying Madeline Hunter's *Mastery Teaching* (1982) model as a "big-picture" framework for integrating the characteristics of adult learning into her planning.

ADAPTING MADELINE HUNTER'S MODEL

For over a decade, Madeline Hunter and her colleagues at the University of California, Los Angeles, studied teaching decisions and their implementation. They came to the conclusion that "*regardless of who or what is being taught* [emphasis added], all teaching decisions fall into three categories:

1. what contents to teach next,

2. what the student will do to learn and to demonstrate learning has occurred, and

3. what the teacher will do to facilitate the acquisition of that learning. (Hunter, 2004, p. 4)

Hunter (2004) also found that if those decisions "also reflect the teacher's sensitivity to the student and to the situation, learning will be increased" (p. 4). To help teachers consciously and deliberately identify the decisions needed to be made in each category, Hunter formulated a set of lesson design elements based on research-validated knowledge. Although they were formulated more than two decades ago, the following elements of Hunter's lesson design are still valid today and, in my opinion and experience, apply to teaching adults as well as children.

1. Purpose and objective

2. Anticipatory set

3. Input

4. Modeling

5. Checking for understanding

6. Closure

Kathy will build her workshop with these elements in mind.

PURPOSE AND OBJECTIVE

> Should you wish either the objective or its . . . purpose to be discovered or a surprise, that is fine. Just be sure that when you don't tell [participants] what they will learn, that is what you intended, rather than having the omission result from your [not being clear about it yourself].
>
> Hunter, 1982, p. 29

Participants need to know up front what they can expect to get out of a workshop and why it will be worth their time to participate. We know that adults are *goal oriented*. They appreciate a program that is organized and has clearly defined elements. Adults are also *relevancy oriented*. They need to feel that the workshop will be applicable to their work and that they will be better teachers, and their students better learners, as a result of their participation. The presenter's first step in planning a workshop, then, is to be crystal clear about *what* participants will learn and *why* they need to learn it.

For example, if the topic of a workshop is "Improving Instruction Through Cooperative Learning," its purpose might be: "to acquire strategies for having students work in small instructional groups in ways that can make instructional time in the classroom more productive and rewarding." The objectives of such a workshop might specify that participants will learn and be able to apply strategies to

1. assign students to groups

2. clarify group activities

3. actively involve all group members

4. hold students accountable both for what they learn as individuals and for the success of other members of the group, and

5. monitor and assess group effectiveness.

I was not being arbitrary, by the way, when I chose to use cooperative learning in the classroom as an example here. Small group activity is an effective methodology for workshop presentations as well. Working in small groups allows for increased interaction among participants, an important and appreciated dynamic for engaging adults in learning.

Like Kathy, you may find it helpful to reflect on the purpose and objective(s) of your presentation before tackling a more formal design. What is the purpose of your workshop? In what way(s) will attending help participants to improve teaching and learning?

_____

_____

_____

What are the objectives of your workshop? What skills, behaviors, and/or understandings will participants learn and be able to apply?

_____

_____

_____

ANTICIPATORY SET

First impressions are important, and the beginning of your [presentation] is no exception. You have experienced how important first impressions of people or places can be. Research in learning validates that effect.

Hunter, 1982, p. 27

Kathy decides she will make it a point to welcome each person as they enter the room. She will also make sure that the room is set up with enough tables and chairs to accommodate the number of participants. There are several configurations of room setups. The one to use depends on the purpose and format of the presentation. In Resource B, you will find several possible arrangements and a discussion of their purposes and advantages.

Kathy decides to include small group activities in her workshop, so she will have the room set up with separate tables—round tables, if available. Each table will seat four to six, the optimal number for effective group work. A packet of materials including handouts (if not distributed as participants enter the room) and a pad and pencil will be on the tables at each place. An assortment of colored markers, a bowl of fruit or candy, and a few novelty hand toys (for those tactile learners who like to fiddle with objects) will occupy the center of each table.

A rule of thumb observed by many professional speakers goes something like this: *Tell them what you are going to say; say it; then tell them what you said.* Kathy will satisfy the first part of this maxim by going over the workshop's agenda with participants. Doing so will also give Kathy the opportunity to clarify her own expectations and to elicit those of the participants. As discussed in the previous chapter, participants' expectations should be solicited and posted early in the workshop and revisited near its end to determine the extent to which they have been met. The start of the workshop is also the time for Kathy to mention housekeeping concerns. For example, she should let people know when the various break times will be and to point out where the bathrooms and other facilities are if the workshop is being held in a venue that's unfamiliar to the participants.

Kathy can effectively address the element of *anticipatory set* by beginning with an exercise that connects seamlessly with the purpose and objectives of the workshop. Resource C, *Web of Connections,* is an example of such an exercise. The exercise is an adaptation of an activity introduced to me by a colleague, Ed Greene, when he and I were copresenting a workshop for early-childhood program directors in New Jersey, during which participants would be working together in small groups.

A word or two of caution is in order here. First, beginning with an activity—even if it is appropriate to the spirit of the session, as in the above example—may not be wise if doing so impinges on the participants' expectations or the time available to present content. Second, unless you can justify the decision, avoid using an opening activity purely as an "icebreaker." The following exchange on the *www.teacher.net* teachers chatboard clearly illustrates this admonition.

On 10/02/04, KAYLA wrote:
I am conducting teacher workshops next week and I need some ice breaker ideas to set a good atmosphere. Thanks!

On 10/02/04, SGH wrote:
I hate stupid activities (like ice-breakers). Skip them and get to the part I can use tomorrow in my classroom!

On 10/02/04, KEZ wrote:
I am with SGH on this one. Introduce yourself and get on with it. I am a rather shy person. Most ice-breakers have put me on the spot and made want to flee. Teachers usually feel like they had to let something go to attend and don't want to fiddle around with "cutesy" icebreakers.

On 10/02/04, Sister Golden Hair wrote:
Are you a teacher? Teachers hate ice breakers. Start your work shop right on time. And forget icebreakers. . . . Playing silly games and get to know you stuff is just ridiculous. I would walk out then and write a bad evaluation on the presenter.

There are exceptions, of course, but I agree that icebreakers for their own sake are best avoided. What *is* valid, however, are exercises like *Web of Connection* that "herald the work ahead [and] . . . provide the participants with robust cues about what is in store for them . . . Most important, the [exercise will] . . . stimulate and inspire, providing a sense of anticipation that will be rewarded and a challenge that will be fulfilled" (Kaagan 2004, p. 6).

Like Kathy, you may find it helpful, before tackling a more formal design, to consider how you will prepare the room and immediately engage participants. What will be the best room setup for the presentation and its participants?

_____

_____

_____

What would be an effective opening activity and how will you relate that activity to the workshop's purpose and objectives?

Opening activity _____

_____

_____

Relation to workshop _____

_____

_____

INPUT

> . . . We must determine which information is basic or essential to [participants'] understanding of the content or process, then separate that information from information which may be desirable but is supplementary and can be acquired later.
>
> Hunter, 1982, p. 33

Kathy will need to decide the main ideas, processes, and information to include in her presentation. Whatever she includes, she should, of course, frame it (see discussion of framing in Chapter 2) and, as much as possible, use specific examples to illustrate general points. For instance, in addition to explaining why the activity illustrates how a teacher might use mathematics to explore social issues, she should also provide an example, such as developing a demographic chart that participants actually work through. It is also a good idea for her to use activities that she has used in classrooms herself, so that she is talking from experience. Teachers will quickly pick up whether she is talking about something that she's never tried herself.

After such an activity, Kathy can ask participants questions such as: Has anyone tried a task like this one before? Will you tell us about it? How would you adapt this activity for your own classroom? Does this activity prompt anyone to think of a related activity that you could try? These kinds of questions validate participants' expertise and encourage them to reflect on their own teaching. The idea is to use activities to draw out principles, rather than providing principles and hoping teachers will figure out implications on their own.

Incidentally, even though I emphasize the value of using interactive workshop strategies such as small group activities, there are other effective ways for participants to acquire information. Lectures, for example, can be very effective. A well-designed lecture, according to Hunter (2004), "can be adjusted to learners' needs in terms of examples used, pacing, vocabulary, and idea density. A lecture can also be modified on the basis of signals given off by [participants] during the lecture" (p. 47). I personally find it more effective at times to present new information or concepts by means of a lecturette. Judiciously alternating the "show and tell" mode of a lecture with the "constructionist" characteristics of interactive activities usually results in a more balanced and probably more interesting format.

Another way to present information is through the use of visual materials. Visual materials not only present and reinforce information but also add variety to a presentation and resonate with various learning styles. Overhead transparencies and Power-Point™, for example, can be very effective. Prepare these in large, legible text—font size of 28 points at a minimum. Also, use as few words as possible to get the point across.

When preparing handouts, think about whether the use of colored paper may make it easier for participants to find their way through a variety of handouts. Consider whether you want to provide handouts as you go, at the end, or at the beginning of your presentation. Handing out everything at the start may be distracting. Then again, handing things out along the way can use up valuable time and interrupt the flow of the presentation. If you wait until the end, participants may write down notes during the presentation, only to find that it is all being given out at the end. I suggest giving out whatever you can at the start that won't "spoil the fun" for what follows. For example, if you are using some kind of problem-solving task and you provide the solutions at the onset, the whole thing could fall flat. As a general rule, you should plan how each segment of the session will finish; otherwise, it may just die without a sense of completion.

Finally, I find it helpful, when preparing for a presentation, to put together a checklist of materials and equipment (e.g., handouts, computer with PowerPoint™ loaded, overheads, projectors, screen, spare bulbs and extension cords, writing materials, masking tape, etc.). I also find it helpful to use a copy of the agenda, to which I add subtopics and notes, as a working outline for my presentations.

What are the main ideas and information you want to include in your presentation? What are appropriate activities and how might you frame those activities? What materials would support these activities?

Main ideas and information _____

_____

_____

Activities and ways to frame them _____

_____

_____

Materials _____

_____

_____

MODELING

> "Give me an example" is a common request when we are not sure we understand what is meant. A model is one kind of example, one which a [participant] can perceive directly . . . rather than having to rely on memory of some previous learning or experience.
>
> Hunter, 1982, p. 45

Let's eavesdrop on two participants who are just coming out of a presentation. "Can you believe it!" says one to the other. "The workshop was about cooperative learning and how to involve students in discussions, yet all we have done for the past two hours is sit there in rows while the presenter lectured to us from his notes."

Modeling the kind of classroom environment that you are encouraging teachers to develop is a powerful strategy and certainly increases the chances that teachers will try the new approaches in their classrooms. Staying with our example of presenting a workshop about cooperative learning for the moment, it goes without saying that the concept of *modeling* calls for workshop participants to work in small groups. The model becomes even stronger as participants recognize that group activity becomes more effective when during the workshop they:

- receive clear directions,
- know the purpose of the group, and
- have specific ways to contribute to the group activity.

Diagrams, photographs, and case studies or vignettes are also examples of models. An effective model should elicit from a participant comments like, "Oh, I see!" or "OK. Now I get it!" Usually, a model will best reinforce an idea or concept if the model is in sync with the participant's preferred learning style (i.e., visual, auditory, or tactile). Make sure, however, that the model you choose is unambiguous, valid, and illustrative or representative of the principle or process you are presenting. For instance, if you are presenting information about the size of type to use on an overhead transparency, project on the screen both a preferred (32 point) and barely legible (10 point) example.

Of course, I hope that this chapter serves as a model of how to design an effective workshop.

How will your presentation model your objectives? _____

_____

_____

CHECKING FOR UNDERSTANDING

> In attempting to check understanding while teaching, teachers may commit three common errors. The most common is a teacher's ubiquitous, "O.K.?" with assumption that student silence means it is O.K. and they understand . . . What student is going to be brave (or brash) enough to say, "No, it's not O.K., you're going too fast!""
>
> Hunter, 1982, p. 59

There are several ways to take occasional "snapshots" during the course of a workshop to check for understanding along the way. One method is to encourage participants to use a subtle signal (e.g., tugging an ear or tapping the side of a nose) if something is not understood. Other methods include asking participants how they might apply what has just been discussed or having them apply the new learning during the session itself. Kate (and you) will find that such devices will let her know whether to move on or to revisit the point, perhaps using a different approach.

Ultimately, of course, the difference between [understanding] how something should be done and being able to do it is the quantum leap in learning. The springboard for that leap is developed by guided practice accompanied by feedback that gives the learner information about what is correct, what needs to be improved and how to improve performance. (Hunter, 1982, p. 71)

Preferably, workshops should be long enough, possibly take place in a multiple-session format, or include some sort of follow-up opportunity so that such guided practice can occur.

Write in the space below how will you know whether participants are "getting it."

_____

_____

CLOSURE

Toward the end of the workshop session, Kathy will review the posted list of expectations with participants, address any unmet expectations to the extent time permits, and possibly arrange some sort of follow-up to address any others. She will thank everyone for their participation and make herself available to talk with anyone afterward.

The workshop will end as scheduled, but the learning can go on if Kathy sets up the conditions for it to happen. Here are three ways to structure opportunities for postworkshop learning.

1. Foster ongoing collaboration among participants by getting commitments to continue to share information and expertise. Resource D, "Standing Offer" (Kaagan, 2004, pp. 87–88), provides an effective exercise for this purpose.

2. Set up a listserv or group (Yahoo supports such groups. Go to *http://groups.yahoo.com* for details) for those interested in the workshop's topic. A listserv is an Internet communication tool that offers its members the opportunity to post suggestions or questions to a large number of people at the same time. Membership on a listserv or group is restricted by its manager to those people it is designed to serve. When you submit a question or something that you want to share to the listserv or group, your submission is automatically distributed to all of the other people on that list.

3. Follow up with visits to participants' classroom. Even with extended workshop time, research by Showers, Joyce, and Bennett (1987) suggests that whether a teacher actually uses in the classroom a skill learned in a workshop depends significantly on classroom follow-up. A workshop takes place isolated from the participants' classrooms and is concerned with helping participants develop new understandings and learn new skills. Follow-up

activities, on the other hand, take place in the "here and now"—in the classroom—and they are concerned with honing the ability of the teacher to productively apply what was learned during the workshop.

A presenter can provide follow-up assistance by observing in the classroom, offering feedback, posing questions to prompt reflection, and modeling teaching techniques. Such follow-up coaching, however, is a highly specialized skill that requires extensive training and practice. It is not within the purview of this book to elaborate on strategies for coaching, other than to point out its value. Those interested can learn more about teachers collaborating for school-based staff development from the National Staff Development Council (NSDC). Access the NSDC Web site, *www.nsdc.org*, and enter "school-based staff development" in its search box.

Plan your presentation using Exercise 3.1 below. Then use the checklist in Exercise 3.2 to make sure you're ready to roll.

Exercise 3.1   Write your Presentation Plan

Name: _____

Workshop Title: _____

Purpose and objective (what participants will learn, and why they will need to learn it)

Anticipatory set (activities that will prepare participants for the topic and their participation)

Input (the information, materials, activities, and processes that are basic or essential to participants' understanding of the content)

(Continued)

Exercise 3.1   (Continued)

Modeling (activities, behaviors, diagrams, photographs, case studies, vignettes, etc., that illustrate a point, concept, or strategy)

Checking for understanding (strategies for assessing learning and adjusting accordingly)

Closure (ways to end the session and provide opportunities for postworkshop learning)

Exercise 3.2   How Well Have You Prepared?

Now, you're almost ready for your presentation. But first, complete the following self-checklist, and then tend to any details that still need your attention.

Circle the appropriate reply: Y = Yes, N = No, NA = Not Applicable

Have I . . .

gathered relevant information about the participants?	Y	N	NA
decided on the purpose and objectives of my presentation?	Y	N	NA
identified a way of starting that will engage the learners?	Y	N	NA
constructed an agenda?	Y	N	NA
structured the session in a logical and intriguing way?	Y	N	NA
accounted for a variety of learning styles?	Y	N	NA
broken my material into short sections so there are opportunities for questions and discussion?	Y	N	NA
created bridges/transitions for helping learners move from one segment to another?	Y	N	NA
built in variety, surprise, and changes of pace?	Y	N	NA
made sure that I won't be overwhelming the learners with information?	Y	N	NA

(Continued)

Exercise 3.2   (Continued)

prepared myself so I can adapt to unexpected events and needed changes?	Y	N	NA
identified and made arrangements for equipment and other resources?	Y	N	NA
made sure I know how to use any equipment needed during my presentation?	Y	N	NA
made sure I have a plan for monitoring the time?	Y	N	NA
Developed a conclusion related to the purpose and body of the presentation?	Y	N	NA
observed other teachers making presentations?	Y	N	NA
reflected on my own experiences as a participant?	Y	N	NA
considered practicing in front of someone?	Y	N	NA
made a candid inventory of my strengths and the areas where I need improvement?	Y	N	NA

CHAPTER FOUR

Presenting the Workshop

K athy has designed her workshop well, but she knows from her own experiences that content isn't the only thing that counts. How the material is presented can make a big difference in how engaged participants are and how much they take away. As she prepares for her first-ever presentation, Kathy relies on suggestions from veteran presenters like Drew, whose advice can increase the probability that she makes an effective presentation, perhaps even an inspiring one. Here are some of the tips she found in her research.

CONQUER STAGE FRIGHT

Everyone is watching me. . . . I bet some of the teachers aren't sure I'll manage it. I feel like my every move is observed. My legs are shaking—can they see how nervous I am? I've worked hard to get here, and now that I am, I'm not sure I'll be able to pull it off. (Villani, 2005, p. 169)

Feelings of anxiety and nervousness are common to many presenters, even experienced ones. Stage fright originates in the mind and manifests itself in the body through tension, dry mouth, and other physical symptoms. It may be difficult to avoid these symptoms when you care about the success of your presentation, but you can control them and channel them into positive energy. Here are a few techniques to help you relax.

- Inhale slowly and deeply on the count of one. Hold your breath as you mentally count two and three. Exhale on the count of four. Repeat four times *very slowly*. Be aware of your heart and respiration slowing down. When you inhale, do so from the diaphragm; that is, let the air fill your stomach area first, then your chest. When you exhale, force the air up from below, through your chest area, then out.
- Clench your fists tightly. Hold for a five count. Relax them suddenly. Repeat three times. Then let your arms hang at your sides and feel your fingers becoming warm. Finally, shake your hands until they tingle.
- If you are sitting, place your hands under your chair and pull up with your fingers while pressing down with your buttocks. Hold for a count of three and release.

- Think less about how you are doing and more in terms of the participants and their needs and interests.
- Think of your presentation as a conversation. You have conversations all the time. Do you get nervous before a conversation? Most conversations are nonthreatening experiences, just a way for two or more people to communicate something. Approach your presentation as though you were having a conversation, just with a few more people.

OVERCOME THE IMPOSTOR SYNDROME

The "impostor phenomenon" is a self-imposed feeling of inadequacy and a fear that others may discover how little one really knows (Clance, 1985). The syndrome is a natural process that can be experienced by both new and veteran presenters. Even when initial feelings of confusion and inadequacy are dispelled, they may reoccur for presenters as they encounter unexpected problems while presenting.

Kathy can allay these feelings by acting in ways that helped her become an effective classroom teacher. Certainly, preparing a well-designed lesson plan is paramount. A few other strategies that can help Kathy overcome the impostor phenomenon include the following, shared by Barbara and Doug Clarke (1996).

- As you would in a regular classroom, have extra activities up your sleeve in case things take less time than you thought. However, for every activity you plan to use, ask yourself: Why am I doing this activity? What do I hope participants would gain from it? Where does it fit in the overall scheme of things?
- Present the session with enough flexibility to enable you to respond to the needs and interests of participants without straying from your purpose and objectives.
- Arrive early. Give yourself a chance to organize the furniture and equipment in a way that you think best enhances the format of the sessions and general communication. Bring a spare lightbulb and extension cord if you are using any technology.
- Although this may seem trivial, wear clothes that feel comfortable and that you feel good about.

HANDLE DIFFICULT SITUATIONS

One of the greatest worries for inexperienced presenters is: What if I am asked a question to which I don't know the answer? Some of the more common questions (often in the form of statements!) that presenters have been asked over the years include:

Been there, done that. These ideas are nothing new. Ten years ago, we tried all this, and it didn't work then.

That's all very well, but I teach 30 kids (many ESL), and my room couldn't possibly cope with that style of activity.

Given the demands of NCLB (No Child Left Behind), how do you expect me to find time for this?

So how can you handle difficult questions?

- Anticipate. With each thing you plan to do, ask yourself in advance "what awkward questions might I be asked, and how will I deal with them?"
- Listen very carefully to the question, and take care not to assume you know the whole question having heard the first few words.
- If you don't know, admit it.
- Use the classic teacher line: "That's a great question. Does anyone have any thoughts on that?"

On the other side of the coin, you can be the one to take the devil's advocate role. For example, you might say, "Some people might say there is no advantage to teaching students this way over the traditional way. What do you think?" Others will usually jump in and respond favorably. This method can be far more powerful than you giving your own answer.

WHAT NOT TO DO

We have all sat through inservice presentations of greatly varying quality and usefulness. What is it that makes the difference between a presentation that inspires us to deep thought and subsequent action and one that drives us to frustration and that terrible shudder as we realize that we have drifted off to sleep? (Clarke & Clarke, 1996).

Among the features of a disappointing presentation are the following:

- The presenter did lots of talking but didn't get the participants actively involved.
- The speaker used a monotone voice and/or "boring" body language.
- The session was not a good fit with what was advertised.
- The presentation didn't seem to be connected to the day-to-day realities of the audience.

Exercise 4.1 on the following page helps you recall other factors that made presentations disappointing for you.

MAKE AN INSPIRING PRESENTATION

Better yet, let us consider the positive experiences we have enjoyed. It is likely that these experiences are the direct opposite of those you accumulated in Exercise 4.1. For example, many people list the following:

- The presenter knew her topic well and spoke with enthusiasm and passion.
- The presenter got us actively and productively involved several times during the session.
- The presenter showed a real understanding of the many challenges we face in our day-to-day work and provided a number of useful strategies for addressing them.

So if you want your workshop to go well, remember to regard teachers as reflective practitioners who will gain more from your presentation if they are given the chance to relate the session to their everyday classroom and school experiences.

Exercise 4.2 helps you make your own list.

It is also important to make it clear in everything you do how much you value the work of teachers. In fact, many of the teachers in your workshop may have strengths in just the areas

Exercise 4.1   Disappointing Presentations

Think of a professional development presentation you attended in the last few years that you found particularly disappointing. What were the features of the presentation that made it such? List them below.

- _____

- _____

- _____

- _____

- _____

Exercise 4.2   Memorable Presentations

Think of a professional development presentation you went to in the last few years that you found particularly outstanding. What were the features of the presentation that made it so memorable? List them below.

- _____

- _____

- _____

- _____

- _____

that you are exploring. Make it a point to share and value these and to build on them. As the saying attributed to Woodrow Wilson goes, "Use more than the brains you have: use all the brains you can get."

Exercise 4.3 helps you to develop your own strategy.

SOME TIPS AND OBSERVATIONS

Have you ever watched a cat watching a mouse? As long as the mouse remains perfectly still, the cat will nonchalantly lick the back of its paw, yawn, or even wander off. People, too, have difficulty attending to anything that does not change. We tune out background sounds such as air conditioning, although we notice when it shuts down. The same principle applies to a presenter with a monotone voice or to one frozen and immobile behind a podium. Excessive repetition, such as relying on slide after slide, can also have the same effect. We may not lick the back of our hands under such conditions, but like the cat, we may yawn . . . or even wander off. You can keep people's attention for long periods of time by using yourself and your environment as changing focal points.

Manage Yourself

You will find it difficult, if not impossible, to present well if you really don't care to be doing it. So remind yourself of the reasons you are presenting. If you are eager to share what you believe in, you will do so with passion. It will show. You will capture attention without having to force yourself. There are ways, however, that you can enlist your voice and body to support your enthusiasm. Here are a few.

Voice

Vary speed, pitch, and volume. End sentences clearly. Avoid excessive use of *um, er, like,* and *you know.* Stress important words. Project your voice to the back of the room. Use silence strategically.

Body Movement

Avoid fidgeting. When you move, do so with a purpose. Move slightly toward or turn in the direction of a person asking a question.

Exercise 4.3   Principles of Good Practice in Presenting

Participants in a workshop are most likely to benefit from the experience if the presenter applies certain principles of good practice. Below are five of these principles. In the space provided after each principle, list the specific activities, actions, or behaviors you will apply to address that principle.

Good practice involves interaction among participants.
Learning is enhanced when it is more like a team effort than a solo race. Working with others often increases involvement in learning. Sharing one's ideas and responding to others' improves thinking and deepens understanding.

I will provide opportunity for participant interaction by:

Good practice uses active learning techniques.
Learning is not a spectator sport. Participants do not learn as much just sitting and listening to the presenter. They must talk about what they are learning, write reflectively about it, relate it to past experiences, and practice ways to apply it to their teaching.

I will use specific active learning techniques to support the following activities in these ways:

Good practice provides timely feedback.
Knowing what you know and don't know focuses your learning. Both presenters and participants benefit from opportunities to assess their understanding. They need opportunities to perform, reflect on their performance, and discover or receive suggestions for improvement.

I will periodically assess participant understanding through the following means:

Good practice emphasizes time on task.
Participants come to presentations to learn. Activities are planned and carried out with that purpose constantly in mind.

I will rely on the following method(s) to keep myself and participants on task:

Good practice respects individuals' varied experiences and unique ways of learning.
Participants need opportunities to demonstrate their expertise and to effectively relate it to new learning.

I will encourage participants to describe and relate to their relevant expertise by:

Good practice communicates high expectations.
Expect both yourself and the participants to learn and to perform well, and your expectations will become a self-fulfilling prophecy.

I will communicate high expectations for participant success by:

Vary distance between yourself and the audience, but do so prudently. For example, step slightly forward when giving a direction; step slightly back while waiting for participants to follow the direction. Modify your facial expressions to fit context.

Eyes

Make frequent eye contact with people; look for friendly faces!

1. Lock your eyes on one person before starting a sentence or thought.

2. Move your eyes around the room, but complete a thought with each individual whose gaze you engage.

3. Pause and breathe while moving to another person.

Gestures

Control your gestures. Practice in front of a mirror. Where are your hands? Keep your hand gestures above your waist; don't let them flutter unnecessarily. Don't twist a ring, crack your knuckles, bite your lip, push your glasses up repeatedly—unless that's what you want your audience to notice! Judiciously punctuate words with arm and hand movements; for example:

- Use palms up to reinforce a question or invitation
- Hold up three fingers when saying "three key ideas"
- Applaud to recognize an insightful statement

General Appearance

Wear clothing that will not detract from your message. You want participants to focus on you and what you are presenting, not on a flamboyant tie or a large, shiny rhinestone pin.

Manage the Environment

Plan ahead. You can avoid distractions by anticipating and removing them. You can focus attention on your message by using well-designed and straightforward material.

Arrive Early

Check the setup ahead of time. Will you want a glass of water handy? Is there enough space for your materials so they won't get out of order? Does the overhead projector work? Is it focused, clean, and the right distance from the screen?

Format Crisp Handouts

- Incorporate fewer rather than more pages, printed legibly on one side, using at least 12-point type.
- Leave space between items for notes.
- Include a cover page, perhaps incorporating an appropriate graphic.
- Number the pages.

Produce Interesting Flip Charts

Prepare pages on your flip chart ahead of time. For example, even though you will write on the newsprint during the session, lightly pencil in key words to help you remember. Illustrations can add interest to a flip chart if used judiciously. If you aren't confident about your own artistic ability, Miravia *(http://www.miravia .com/04_01.htm)*, for example, carries a product called ChartArt consisting of 32 line-art images that can be lightly traced in ahead of time and overdrawn later with a marker. Here are some other flip chart suggestions.

- Prepare material on every other page so that you have a blank page ready if needed.
- Use two or three different colored markers.
- Limit what you write on a sheet to key words only, written large enough to be seen by all.

Use Music

Music is an incredibly powerful instructional tool which can be added to most . . . learning situations . . . Properly employed, it can create a heightened social context, motivate [participants] to engage themselves more rapidly, and provide a sense of safety that might not otherwise be possible. (Allen, 2005, p. 30)

Match the music to the activity. Here are some effective times to use music:

- Before the workshop or activity formally begins, music sets the tone for the session. Also, decreasing the volume or stopping it altogether signals the start of the activity.
- During movement, music should match the tempo of the activity.
- During discussions, music, softly played, provides a comfortable background to conversations between and among participants.
- After the workshop, music can provide participants with a positive image of the session as they gather materials and prepare to leave.

Manage the Presentation

Know your material. (*Never* read it!). Open your presentation with a few remarks or a bit of humor to give people time to settle in and get their minds focused.

Start and End on Time

If there is some reason to start late, don't start with an apology. Greet the group first, commend them for something, apologize quickly, tell participants when you expect to start, and give them something to do, such as reading a handout, while they wait. End when advertised, not later. Plan to be available for a while afterward to speak with individuals.

Highlight Key Points

Present major points in memorable ways. People may not see the relevance of what is being said without the implications being teased out for them. A powerful way to highlight is to link the fact or piece of information to a related benefit. It is important that the presenter understand the concerns of the audience with respect to the topic and address them early. Always establish relevance from the point of view of the participants! You can help participants focus on key points through verbal emphasis (tone, loudness, silence) and the use of overheads, handouts, and flip charts.

Simplify Directions

Give directions one at a time, and wait until each item has been accomplished before giving the next one. Most people will lose track of what you ask them to do if they have to remember several directions at once. For example, what response would you expect from the following?

Please stand, then go over to the table and choose a paper from one of the piles, bring the paper back to your seat, write your name on the top right corner, answer questions one to six, then discuss your answers with your partner.

A better way is to begin the sequence with "Please stand." Wait until everyone is on their feet, then continue with, "There are several piles of paper on the table. In a moment, when I say 'go,' go to the table, take one sheet from any of the piles, and return to your seat."

Avoid Lethal Blunders

- Arrogance: acting like a "know-it-all" expert.
- Ignorance: being unaware of local culture and tradition.
- Tactlessness: telling off-color jokes and using racist, sexist, or derogatory language.
- Insensitivity: mocking or embarrassing a participant.
- Misjudgment: ignoring the needs, makeup, and level of expertise of participants.

Finally, remember: It's not about you. Yes, it is natural at first to center your concern on your own performance, but as soon as you can, shift your focus to the participants and their concerns; you will all benefit from doing so and will enjoy the experience much more! Use Exercise 4.4 to assess how your presentation went.

Exercise 4.4   How Did It Go?

When your presentation is over and you've had time to relax, it's a good idea to reflect on whether you've carried out everything you planned; if not, why not; and to consider where you need to improve the next time you make a presentation. The following self-checklist will help you do this.

Circle the appropriate reply: Y = Yes, N = No, NA = Not Applicable

At the beginning of my presentation, did I . . .

introduce myself and greet the participants?	Y	N	NA
gather (more) information about the participants?	Y	N	NA
project a sense of purpose, positive anticipation, and enthusiasm?	Y	N	NA
capture the learners' interest?	Y	N	NA
share with participants the purpose and agenda of the session?	Y	N	NA

During my presentation, did I . . .

create an atmosphere of trust?	Y	N	NA
make eye contact with participants?	Y	N	NA
use natural gestures?	Y	N	NA
avoid distracting dress and mannerisms?	Y	N	NA
use the pitch and volume of my voice effectively?	Y	N	NA
deliver material in a clear, energetic way?	Y	N	NA

use humor?	Y	N	NA
model and show learners something rather than just telling them about it?	Y	N	NA
use handouts and audiovisuals effectively?	Y	N	NA
ask questions and give participants a chance to respond?	Y	N	NA
respond to participants' nonverbal messages (e.g. puzzlement, fatigue)?	Y	N	NA
vary what I did?	Y	N	NA
monitor the time?	Y	N	NA

At the end of the presentation, did I . . .

avoid introducing new points in the last few minutes of the session?	Y	N	NA
summarize what I thought had been accomplished or ask learners to do so?	Y	N	NA
prepare participants for what, if anything, they need to do before the next session?	Y	N	NA
determine whether the participants had any lingering questions, concerns, or expectations?	Y	N	NA
end the session with good energy?	Y	N	NA
invite or arrange for feedback, either at the end of the session or sometime following the session?	Y	N	NA

CHAPTER FIVE

Growing as a Presenter

K athy and Justin were having their usual before-school coffee in the teachers room. "Georgette told me," said Kathy, "that during a conference she attended last week, she told other administrators about how successful the workshop I presented was." Kathy took a business card from her pocket and handed it to Justin. "A superintendent gave Georgette this and asked her to have me contact him about presenting the workshop for teachers in his district."

Justin read the card. "Wow! This is a superintendent of a large school district in another state." He handed the card back to Kathy. "Are you going to do it?"

"You bet. Georgette encouraged me to contact the superintendent and express my interest in presenting to his staff. Georgette said she would support me in any way she could, including giving me a professional day off, if necessary, but that she had no money available to pay any of my expenses . . . I would have to negotiate that with the superintendent, who, by the way, told Georgette he expects to pay the presenter a fee."

Kathy contacted the superintendent and received a favorable reply. She subsequently successfully presented a workshop to teachers and administrators in the superintendent's district. Over the next couple of years, Kathy presented several workshops in her own district and others.

FREELANCING

Kathy will reach retirement age at the end of the current school year. She wants to remain active in education in some capacity. She wants to do so in a way that would allow her to pass on her considerable experience to other teachers. Kathy remembers how professionally stimulating and personally gratifying her presenting experiences have been. She decides to prepare now for the opportunity to present and facilitate workshops after retirement. Here are some of the issues and concerns facing Kathy. You, too, will face these issues when you decide to turn pro.

- How will you market your availability and advertise your presentations?
- What financial arrangements and obligations are appropriate?
- Should presentations be evaluated? If so, how and why?

MARKETING

If you expect to be hired as a presenter, consultant, or facilitator, people need to know

- about you and how to contact you, and
- why they should hire you.

Advertise your expertise and availability. You won't be asked to present, consult, or facilitate if people don't know about you and what you have to offer. Like several of my fellow presenters and consultants, I found that word-of-mouth was and still is our best marketing device. However, for those of you just starting out, relying on word-of-mouth can be a catch 22; that is, few people are able to recommend you because only a few have seen you in action. But as the number and quality of your presentations grow, so will the number and quality of referrals. Meanwhile, there are some other tried-and-true marketing strategies that you might consider.

Business Cards

The purpose of your business card is to reinforce your introduction to a person and to encourage that person to remember and contact you. Business cards should be simple and to the point: name, address, e-mail, Web page URL, fax, and a one to three word title (e.g., Education Consultant). Avoid cutesy illustrations or cartoons, although a simple, appropriate line drawing can be effective. Graphic designers, printing establishments, and copy centers prepare business cards, or you can create your own using any of several inexpensive software programs, such as PrintShop.

Brochures

The purpose of your brochure is to inform its readers about what you do and how what you do can help them. It should also show potential clients how to contact you and encourage them to do so.

Write your brochure copy from the potential client's point of view, not yours. Yes, they will want to know about you and your expertise, but more important, they are interested in how you can address their needs. Don't present yourself as an expert in more than one or two specific areas. Focus on your niche and what you can contribute in that area. Include short, signed testimonials if you have them.

Professional graphic designers can produce an attractive bifold or trifold brochure (or a single-page flyer) for you, or you can create your own. Computer software programs such as PrintShop, Adobe Pagemaker, and Microsoft Publisher provide templates for crafting brochures and flyers. If you do create your own, keep it simple. Here are some hints:

- Use a one page, bifold, or trifold format; not more.
- Include only pertinent information, and present it simply.
- Include not more than two or three sentences per paragraph.
- Keep text lines short.
- Use boldface type sparingly to emphasize key points.
- Leave adequate margins on all four sides.
- Avoid clichés and jargon.

Exercise 5.1 can help you get started.

Write an Article or Book

Being published, especially in a respected professional journal or by a well-regarded publisher, adds credibility and name recognition to your marketing efforts. If the published work provides information as to where you may be contacted, all the better.

If you are not published, the next best thing is to be mentioned in an article or book written by someone else.

By the way, think twice about including your e-mail address in a book. I have done so to encourage contact from potential clients and then changed my Internet service provider (ISP). E-mail sent to my old ISP address now gets lost in cyberspace. Some publishers maintain a speakers bureau through which they arrange contacts between their authors and potential clients. This book's publisher, Corwin Press, invites authors to be included in its speakers bureau *(http://www.corwinpress.com/speakersbureau/speakershome.aspx)*.

Create a Personal Web Site

A personal Web site serves as an electronic brochure with the added feature that it can easily be kept up-to-date. You can hire a

Exercise 5.1   Plan Your Brochure or Flyer

What does an effective brochure look like? Do some research and reflection.

1. Look at a brochure or flyers that got your attention recently. Is it easy to tell who the brochure or flyer is from and how to find or contact them?   ____Yes   ____No

2. If you answered 'Yes' to Question 1, what is it that makes identity and contact information stand out, and how? If you answered 'No' how would you improve upon what was done?

    Placement? _____

    Size? _____

    Type style/color? _____

    Other? _____

3. List one to three additional features of a brochure or flyer that caught your eye in a favorable way.

4. List one to three aspects of the brochure or flyer that you ignored or found unnecessary.

5. Draft the information and features that would make your brochure or flyer effective.

Contact information:

Information about you:

What you offer the target client:

References or testimonials:

Other information:

Notes regarding layout, color, graphics, size, etc.:

professional Web page designer, or you can create and manage your own page. There are several commercial and self-help Web design possibilities. Use a search engine, such as Google. Type in words such as "create web page," and you will probably call up scores of possibilities. I created and manage my personal Web site (www.portner.us/Hal) using the FrontLine program in MicroSoft Office.

Contact Regional Education Service Providers

Many states or consortiums of school districts maintain education centers (e.g., BOCES in New York State and ESCs in Texas) that, among other services, provide staff development workshops for their member schools. Meet with the service center's professional development coordinator to explore the possibility of making presentations under its auspices. State Department of Education Web sites often provide Internet links to the service centers in their states.

Present at Conferences

Presenting a session at a regional or national conference is a great way to introduce others to your expertise and presentation skills. Proposals to present are usually due well in advance of the actual conference—often 8 to 10 months. The World Wide Web pages of most professional associations often provide information about proposing to present at their upcoming conference. For example, here is some of what the National Staff Development Council's (NSDC) current proposal submission form contains.

NSDC Proposal Tips

Your abstract should give a clear picture of the participants learning as a result of the session as well as a preview of the processes you will use. Please write in active voice.

Participant outcomes should be statements of the knowledge and skills participants will have at the end of your session, not what the participants will do during the session.

Cite research that specifically supports your proposal.

Incomplete proposals will not be accepted.

If the "beginning" level is selected for your audience, participants will leave with either new knowledge or skills. A "deeper understanding" applies only to regular and advanced sessions.

The deadline for proposals is final.

Consider submitting "advance" sessions. These are in high demand and few quality proposals are received each year. This is also true of sessions using the Book Talk and Conversation formats.

NSDC awards extra points in the scoring process for sessions presented by school- and district-based practitioners. If you are from an organization that supports schools you are encouraged to submit your proposal with a second presenter representing a school or district partner.

Even if you do not present at a conference, the information and networking opportunities resulting from attending can be invaluable.

Write Captivating and Accurate Workshop Descriptions

There may be times when your workshop is one of several concurrent sessions, or it may be competing for participants in some other way. Even when your workshop is the only one being offered, people want to know not only its content but also something about what to expect. Here is what one teacher told me: "I want an extremely clear description of the intent of the workshop, especially who should attend. Vague descriptions have caused me to waste *hours* waiting for the 15 minutes that would apply to me."

- Make the title straightforward and precise.
- Get to the point right from the first sentence.
- State clearly who should attend and why.
- Highlight what participants can expect to get out of the session.
- Keep descriptions jargon free and light on philosophy.

Here is an example of a well-crafted workshop description.

How to Teach Reading to Low-Achieving 3rd, 4th, & 5th Graders

Length: 6 hours

Learn how to ensure that your students are getting the basics of reading. You will return to your classroom from this fast-paced and fun seminar with the knowledge and instructional strategies you need to begin to turn reading failure into reading success for all your students, especially your struggling readers.

You will learn how to incorporate the 10 essential elements of reading success into your existing program. When you leave this outstanding workshop, you will be able to:

Meet the needs of the wide range of reading abilities in your classroom without adding stress to your day

Ensure continuous progress for fluent and struggling readers alike by enhancing your current reading program

Increase comprehension and word attack skills

Increase reading skills by utilizing outstanding children's literature (fiction and non-fiction)

GUARANTEEING SUCCESS

Why should you be the one asked to present, coach, or facilitate rather than someone else? Because you convince the potential client not only that you have the skills and experience they want but also that you know their needs and are able to effectively address those needs—that's how! Just as you personalize the cover letter you send with a résumé, and just as you do your research before showing up for a job interview, you target your message to the potential client.

Know Your Audience

Several years ago I was contracted to present a 2-day workshop on mentoring new teachers. My contact person told me that I should concentrate on teaching mentoring skills. Without following up with specific questions about the participants' expertise as mentors, I wrongly assumed they were beginners and designed my presentation accordingly. Disaster! It turned out they all had at least one full year's experience as mentors, had gone through formal mentor training, and participated in monthly mentor networking session. They were bored stiff, and the second day was cancelled.

People come to your presentation attracted by a captivating workshop description or by your reputation, but there's no guarantee they will walk away satisfied. It is critical that you know the level of their understanding, skills, and experience regarding the content of your topic *prior* to finalizing the workshop design—or at the very least, before the presentation itself. This may mean a phone call or two and/or a series of e-mails. Ask questions. Probe for details. Don't assume. For example, if you are contacted by a potential client about conducting a workshop, find out

- Who will attend? Then you can indicate how and where you worked successfully with similar groups.
- How much expertise regarding your topic do participants already have? Then you can acknowledge their experience, indicate your understanding of their needs, and stress your ability to meet them.
- What do the client and participants expect to gain from your session? Then you can offer practical results as well as discuss "big picture" outcomes.

Specialize

Find your niche and stick to it. Become known and respected as an expert in a specific area. I would question the depth of knowledge of a presenter who offers to personally present a workshop on any of half a dozen topics. For example, I recently came across the following anonymous request on a teacher's chatboard:

> I am in the process of preparing a series of lectures/seminars, and I am looking for what teachers out there would be interested in. Art? Sensory experiences? Language? Classroom management? Better parent communication? Please let me know of any topics or others . . . I would like to meet the needs of teachers out there. Thank you all

Does this person intend to "meet the needs of [ALL] teachers out there," by himself or herself? If so, chances are that few if any of the topics offered will be thoroughly presented. Savvy administrators know this and would be reluctant to engage such a presenter. If, on the other hand, the intent of the person posting the request is to put together a group of presenters, each expert in a particular area, then the results can be positive.

Should You Copresent?

Consider presenting with a partner. It goes without saying that the two of you must not only trust and respect each other but also be able to work together in mutually supportive ways. For example, copresenters should agree beforehand whether it is okay for one to interrupt the other to add to or reinforce a point.

There are several advantages to copresenting. Copresenting presents opportunities for adding variety to the proceedings. For example, I have copresented with people of different gender and ethnicity from my own and found that, together, we connected favorably with more participants than might otherwise have been possible. Participants also appreciate the back-and-forth change from one style to another. Here are some other advantages.

- Share ideas and tasks
- Get a chance to rest during the presentation
- Learn from each other (be critical friends)
- Provide opportunity to debrief

FEES AND FINANCES

What fee should you ask? This is a concern that causes a fair amount of consternation for many novice presenters. When asked, veteran presenters or facilitators will usually answer "whatever their budget allows" or "find out the going rate, and charge that." I tend to say it depends on your experience, content, and skills. Here is what I suggest.

- If you are just starting out, "know your stuff" but are not yet experienced enough to feel you can present it exceptionally well, and are as much concerned about your performance as you are with the participants' learning, then your fee should range from $300 to $600 per day. By "per day" I mean a morning and afternoon session totaling 5 to 8 hours. What should your fee be for a half day (2 to 4 hours)? If you are close to home and little additional time with the client is involved, $200 to $450 is reasonable; otherwise, charge at your full day's rate.

• If you can offer strong content, excellent material, and good presenting or facilitating skills and experience, and you have established expertise in the area of your presentation or consulting, set your daily fee at $1,000 to $2,000. Jensen (1998) adds what he calls the "top dog" fee-setting range. "These are the career trainers, facilitators and presenters who have all the work they want. Fees range from $2,000 to $7,500 per day. They demand these high honorariums because they can get them. They represent the best in their field; they are household names to their peers" (p. 127).

If you feel embarrassed asking for what may seem an excessive fee, remember that you've spent a lot of time and money preparing for your presentation, and that you have the knowledge and skills to make that presentation inspiring.

You are rather like the repair man who was called upon to fix a nonfunctioning machine. He took a hammer from his tool kit and struck the machine a sharp blow. The machine hummed into life.

The repair man handed the machine's owner a bill for $1,000. The owner was flabbergasted. "$1,000 for two minutes of work? I demand an itemized bill!"

The repairman sighed, wrote out an itemized bill, and handed it to the owner.

Itemized Bill	
Hitting machine with hammer	$ 1.00
Knowing where and how to hit it	$ 999.00
Total	$1,000.00

Establish your fee, make it reasonable, and don't compromise. Granted, there may be circumstances where you would charge less. For example, if you are contracted for multiple consecutive days or for a number of services to be spread over a period of time, a total fee prorated at less than your daily rate is reasonable. You may be tempted to lower your fee to help out a friend or to honor a client's budget restraints; resist the temptation. Consider the message behind this true story.

Years ago, I served as chairman of the Connecticut High School All-State Orchestra Committee. I asked Moshe Paranov, conductor of the Hartford Symphony Orchestra at the time and president of the Hartt College of Music, University of Hartford, to be the All-State Orchestra's guest conductor. Dr. Paranov replied that he would be pleased to do so and that his fee is $2,000.

The Connecticut Music Educators Association had budgeted only $1,000 for the conductor. I informed Dr. Paranov of our budget constraint and asked if he would lower his fee. He reacted as though I had cast aspersions on the memory of his sainted grandmother, kicked his pet dog, and cut off his trademark flowing white hair. "How dare you!" he fumed. I felt the blood drain from my face. "$2,000 is my fee. Do not insult me by asking that I lower it!"

Now understand; this was a highly revered and powerful member of the musical community and a lifelong supporter of music education—and I had insulted him. "I . . . I'm truly sorry, sir, but . . . but I . . ."

"Calm down, son," he said. "I'll tell you what; here are two options. Either you (1) pay me my fee—not a penny less, or (2) ask me to provide my services free and donate the $1,000 you've budgeted to the Hartt College scholarship fund."

I gulped and meekly offered Option 2. He smiled and accepted on the spot, adding, "I look upon my fee with the same passion that I have for my musical performance. I won't compromise either, but I will give both away freely for the right reasons."

Tax Obligations

You are selling a service, and therefore you do not impose and collect a sales or use tax on what you do. You are, however, required to pay an income tax on the fees you earn. I am not a tax lawyer or accountant, nor am I any kind of expert on the subject, so you should check with yours. I can, however, out of personal experience, point out some aspects of income taxes that may apply to you as a freelance consultant and presenter.

- When you work for yourself and are paid a fee, taxes are not withheld, and the tax rate for self-employment earnings applies. Self-employment earnings are taxed at a considerably higher rate than other income, so consider having your taxes professionally prepared.
- You would be well advised to set aside a portion of your fees for income taxes. Also, you should pay quarterly estimated taxes. I am not certain, but you may be required by law to do so.
- The good news is that many of your expenses are tax deductible if you itemize. These deductions include preparation and production cost of materials; purchase and repair costs of related equipment; office equipment and supplies; related travel, meals, lodging, publications, and postage; professional conference fees; and advertising.

EVALUATING A WORKSHOP

Usually, the client or sponsoring organization will hand out and collect at the end of a workshop an "evaluation form" that asks participants to rate the session and the presenter's performance (Resource E, Workshop Evaluation, is an example of such a form). Evaluation forms may also ask how the participant intends to apply "back home" what was learned in the workshop. Ideally, however, the workshop evaluation ought to contribute to the learning process of both the presenter and participants.

Contribute to the learning process? What can evaluation have to do with the learning process? Plenty! Unfortunately, when an outside presenter is brought in to present at a school or people from a number of schools gather for a regional session, there is usually no opportunity to follow up or otherwise reinforce participant learning or for the presenter to assess the effectiveness of the presentation. To me, the value of a workshop is not what people think a few minutes after the formal end of the session. Rather, an honest and useful evaluation means finding out a few days, weeks, or even months down the road what participants are or are not doing differently as a result of the session and what effect their participation is having on the teaching and learning process.

One way you can carry out such long-term evaluation is to collect e-mail addresses of participants, set up a group address block on your computer, and later, e-mail the set of participants asking for replies to a series of questions.

Another way I have used effectively is to give each participant (1) an envelope that they address to themselves; (2) a letter (see Resource F for an example) on which they may write some notes, if they wish, and that they fold and place in the envelope; and (3) another envelope, unsealed, stamped, and addressed to me, that they also place in the first envelope. They then seal the envelope they have addressed to themselves and hand the envelope to me. I mail it to them on a predetermined date, usually a month or two after the workshop. The letter asks that they complete some information and mail it back to me in the enclosed self-addressed stamped envelope. In addition to soliciting information that helps me learn, the letter contributes to participants' learning by prompting them to revisit the workshop material and reflect on its application. Here is an example of replies I received from one such evaluation letter after a series of 10 peer-coaching workshops I presented for teachers and professional staff of a Grade 3-to-6 elementary school in western Massachusetts.

We, as a staff, have endured many changes in leadership and direction over the past several years amidst ever growing pressures to align curriculum and improve test scores. Those transitions and pressures had taken their toll on us as individuals and as a group. This workshop series was offered as we began yet another transition in leadership (note: a new principal was scheduled to arrive in August; the sixth principal in the past 12 years). There existed hope for the future, but a fair amount of exasperation as well. It was time for the healing to begin and a time to reenergize so that we could meet the needs of each other as well as our charges. It was an opportunity to join with our colleagues, to remind ourselves of our mission, to feel part of a team, to reacquaint ourselves with many and diverse assets, and to renew our commitment to professional growth as a staff.

Kevin W., counselor, Grades 3 to 6

Teaching can be a very isolated profession. Peer-coaching allows me the opportunity for professional growth and creativity while being supported by my peers—a new experience for me after 18 years of teaching.

Maggi G., teacher, Grade 4

I am beginning to feel the support building throughout our school community, and I feel comfortable now asking colleagues with strengths I admire to observe my teaching practices. Just the fact that we feel safe and supported when we are in each other's rooms is like a breath of fresh air.

Janet D., teacher, Grade 6

I have had the pleasure of working with and appreciating the skills of one of our district's best teachers. We have always enjoyed each other's company but have rarely had a chance to see each other teach. Realizing that even the most seasoned veterans (we've both taught for 26 years) need support as much as the new teachers is a big step for any district. It has given us a way to collect and interpret data in a way that fosters listening skills, reflection, and has led to meaningful professional growth in other areas as well.

Michele H., teacher, Grade 4

Finally, becoming an effective and sought after presenter, trainer, or consultant takes time, energy, and practice. Stick to it and work hard at it. It will all be worth the effort once you have lived through the experience, tasted its success, and realized that both you and your program's participants have grown as a result.

Resource A

Learning Style Inventory
Or Discovering How You Learn Best

H uman beings possess five senses—seeing, hearing, feeling, tasting, and smelling. We use these senses to acquire information about the world around us. But we do not all necessarily rely on these senses in the same way or to the same degree. This is also true in the acquisition of knowledge.

To gain a better understanding of yourself as a learner you need to evaluate the way you prefer to learn. The following evaluation, based on the *Barsch Learning Style Inventory,* is a short, quick way of assessing your learning style.

ASSESSING YOUR LEARNING STYLE

Place a check on the appropriate line after each statement.

	Often	Sometimes	Seldom
1. I can remember more about a subject through listening than reading.	_____	_____	_____
2. I follow written directions better than oral directions.	_____	_____	_____
3. I like to write things down or take notes for later review.	_____	_____	_____

(Continued)

(Continued)

	Often	Sometimes	Seldom
4. I bear down extremely hard with pen or pencil when writing.			
5. I need oral explanations of charts, diagrams, graphs, or other visual materials.			
6. I enjoy working with tools.			
7. I am skillful with, and enjoy developing or making, charts, graphs, and diagrams.			
8. I can tell if sounds match when presented with a pair of sounds.			
9. I remember best by writing things down several times.			
10. I can easily understand and follow directions on maps.			
11. I do better at academic subjects by listening to lectures and tapes.			
12. I play with coins or keys in my pockets or fidget with objects in my hands.			
13. I learn to spell better by repeating the letters out loud than by writing the word on paper.			
14. I can better understand a news article by reading it in the paper than by listening to the radio.			
15. I like to chew gum, smoke, or snack while studying.			
16. I feel the best way to remember something is to picture it in my head.			
17. I learn spelling by tracing or "finger spelling" the words.			
18. I would rather listen to a good lecture or speech than read about the same material in a textbook.			
19. I am good at working and solving jigsaw puzzles, mazes, etc.			
20. I like to grip objects in my hands during study periods.			
21. I prefer to listen to the news on the radio rather than reading about it in the newspaper.			

22. I obtain information on an
    interesting subject by reading   _____   _____   _____
    relevant materials.

23. I feel comfortable touching others,   _____   _____   _____
    hugging, handshaking, etc.

24. I can follow spoken directions better   _____   _____   _____
    than written ones.

Often = 5 points
Sometimes = 3 points
Seldom = 1 point

DETERMINING YOUR PREFERENCE SCORE

Match your responses to the questions above with the corresponding item number below. Place the point value on the line next to the number. Finally, add the points in each column to obtain the preference scores under each heading. For example, if you responded to Question 1 with a *Sometimes,* then place a three (3) beside the No. 1 in the middle column.

VISUAL		AUDITORY		TACTILE	
No.	Points	No.	Points	No.	Points
2	___	1	___	4	___
3	___	5	___	6	___
7	___	8	___	9	___
10	___	11	___	12	___
14	___	13	___	15	___
16	___	18	___	17	___
20	___	21	___	19	___
22	___	24	___	23	___
VPS =		APS =		TPS =	

VPS = Visual Preference Score
APS = Auditory Preference Score
TPS = Tactile Preference Score

Adapted with permission from the *Learning Style Inventory* developed (1995) by Richard L. Oliver, PhD, Student Learning Assistance Center, San Antonio College, San Antonio Texas. The original inventory can be accessed on the Internet: http://www.accd.edu/sac/slac/handouts/Studyaids/sskills_aid_3.htm

Resource B

Seating Arrangements for Learning Environments

Note: Even if the activities of the learning session do not require changing the seating rearrangements occasionally, there are several reasons to do so:

- Learners are given a new perspective on the activity by sitting in a different part of the room.
- They get better acquainted with their peers.
- Learners are not consistently "punished" by being at greater distances from the screen or speakers.
- Small cliques do not arise—there is nothing wrong with cliques but in some cases they can become a problem by forcing their norms or agendas upon the entire group.

Traditional Seating—Best used for short lectures to large groups

```
O O O O O O O
O O O O O O O
O O O O O O O
O O O O O O O
O O O O O O O
        X
```

- Communication tends to be one way
- Trainer cannot see the learners in the back

Modified Traditional—There is more participation

```
O O O O      O O O O
O O O O      O O O O
O O O O      O O O O
O O O O  O O O O
 O O O O  O O O O
```

X

- Allows the trainer to see all the learners
- Reduces space between trainer and learners as trainer can move up aisle
- Best used for short lectures to large groups

Horseshoe—Nonverbally encourages participation by allowing eye contact between the trainer and all the learners

```
O O O O O
O        O
O        O
O        O
   X
```

- The trainer is able to move closer to each learner
- Works well when all learners must be able to see a demonstration
- Works well when learners will be involved in large group discussions

---

Modular—Learners can work in small groups on exercises and projects

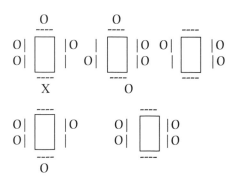

- Communication between trainer and learners is more difficult
- Trainer must move between groups during lectures and activities
- Good for courses that require a lot of group work

Circle—Most democratic and unencumbered with no status symbol

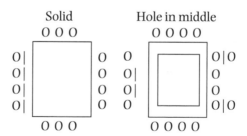

- With no table each person is "totally revealed"
- Subtle nonverbal communications are possible
- There will be conversations, shorter inputs, and more members will participate when they sit at a round table rather than at a square table

---

Square—More formality than a circle

Solid	Hole in middle
O O O	O O O O
O| O O	O|O
O| O O|	O
O| O O|	O
O| O O	O|O
O O O	O O O O

- Nobody can see all the faces of the other participants
- Depending where visual aids are placed, one side may become the "head of the table"
- A solid table seems to encourage conversation
- With a hole in the middle, some people do not speak at all, and some who do speak tend to talk for longer periods of time

---

Rectangle: Fewer people can communicate face-to-face

- The seats at the short dimensions of the table are often seen as leadership positions (because the father sat at the head?)
- If used, the learners should be forced to take distinctly different positions every now and then (i.e. randomly shift the name cards)

Scatter shot: Seems extremely haphazard but good for experiential training

- Permits quick change of learner focus
- Produces tremendous investments of learner energy
- Works well with multiple role plays
- Can quickly form into large groups
- Bad for note taking

Used with permission. Copyright 1997 by Donald Clark http://www.nwlink .com/~donclark/hrd.html

Resource C

Web of Connections

PURPOSE

- To introduce participants to each other
- To illustrate the potential for enjoyment as well as shared responsibility inherent in collaboration

CONTEXT AND DURATION

The exercise should take place at the beginning of the workshop. Depending on the number of participants, the activity will take about 15 or 20 minutes.

PROPS

A ball of string containing enough string to create a web when extended from participant to participant back and forth across a circle. A separate ball of string is needed for each group of more than eight people.

PROCEDURE

Participants face each other (either seated or standing) in a circle. Separate circles are formed for each group of about eight. The first person in each circle holds the end of the string, says "My name is XXXXX and I teach XXXXX." While still holding the end of the string, he or she tosses the ball of string to a person across the circle, leaving a trail of string between the two. The person catching the ball says "Thank you, XXXXX. I am YYYY and teach YYYYY." The second person then holds on to the string and tosses the ball to a third person. The process continues until everyone has caught and passed on the ball of string, and the last person tosses the ball back to person No. 1. The web is formed something like this.

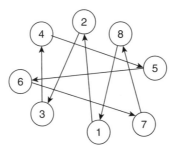

Members of the group describe their thoughts and feelings about sustaining the web by maintaining just enough tension, but not destroying it by applying too much. Then the person (Person 1) holding the ball of string is told to let go of the string and ball. That person and the rest of the group describe their thoughts and feelings about "dropping the ball" and no longer contributing to the group's task.

Note: Groups can take this exercise to another level by including in their ball of string, variations of color and texture (e.g., a combination of heavy string, lightweight (thin) rope, scarves, etc.) to further the analogy about different types of connections and viewpoints that can develop during group work.

Resource D

Standing Offer

PURPOSE AND RATIONALE

This last exercise is meant to foster trust among participants. It invites participants to position their professional relationships around common commitments. For some participants, this exercise presents the possibility of a fresh start; for others, the potential for expanded collaboration. The simple axiom at work here is that cooperation is built when all participants have to extend themselves past the halfway mark in their relationships with colleagues.

CONTEXTUAL CUES

This exercise is not an opener. Rather, it should be inserted when participants have achieved a degree of common ground, i.e., have reached tentative agreement on a joint agenda for improved teaching and learning in the school.

DURATION

The exercise takes about half an hour, including postactivity discussion.

OPTIMAL GROUP SIZE

A group of 12 to 20 works best, although it can be done with larger groups if divided into smaller groups whose members work together.

PROPS

An easel with newsprint sheets and Magic Markers.

PREPARATION

A dash of forethought on the part of all participants.

PROCESS

At an appropriate juncture in one of the concluding development sessions, each participant presents a verbal "standing offer" to the whole group. The offer should relate to the emerging agenda of the group regarding improved teaching and learning schoolwide. The offer could be the provision of expert advice to colleagues in an area where the participant is expert. It could be a tangible contribution to a schoolwide learning theme, such as a display of photographs or artifacts from a recent overseas experience. It could be anything, as long as it advances the common cause.

When all participants have made an offer, each pairs off with a colleague whose offer runs along similar lines. Pairs discuss the offers in more detail, focusing specifically on how they can ensure that they are implemented and honored.

After these brief discussions, the whole group reconvenes to address the questions that follow.

QUESTION FOR REFLECTION

1. What was the overall effect of this activity?

2. How might we characterize the spirit in which it was conducted?

3. To what extent will the sum total of the offers advance our common agenda?

4. To what extent did the exercise open up new opportunities for collaboration between us as school professionals?

5. What difference did it make that we paired off to discuss the offers?

6. What have we learned about effective approaches to assessing the extent to which the offers are implemented and achieve their intended effects?

7. How might this exercise be adapted to a teacher's work with students?

Resource E

Workshop Evaluation

Please check: __ Teacher   __ Administrator   __ Professor
               __ Coordinator   __ Instructional   __ Consultant
                                    Coach
               __ Staff Developer   __ Paraprofessional   __ Other

Overall Impression	*Excellent (comments)*	*Good (comments)*	*Fair (comments)*	*Poor (comments)*
Program content				
Program format and organization				
Presenter's knowledge of subject				
Presenter's ability to engage participants				

(Continued)

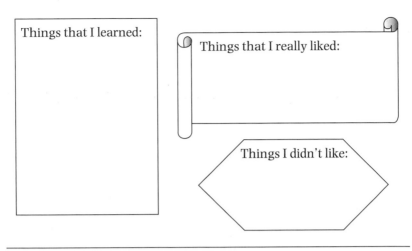

Things that I learned:

Things that I really liked:

Things I didn't like:

Resource F

Evaluation Letter

(Date to be mailed)

Dear (participant writes in his or her name)

Two months ago, you along with several of your ___[school or district here]___ colleagues, joined me at ___[event]___ for dinner and dialogue. The event, arranged by the ___[organization]___, focused on "___[topic of meeting]___."

We examined the _____.
We discussed issues of _____.
We touched on _____.

Now, I would very much appreciate some follow-up reflection and information regarding the impact of that event on your experiences to date. Please take a few minutes to think about how our ___[date of session]___ session may have influenced your understanding of _____ and your ability to function more effectively as a result.

Please write your comments on the back of this page (use an additional sheet of paper if necessary), and mail this letter and any other relevant material you may care to send me in the enclosed stamped/addressed envelope. I truly am interested in your comments and may want to quote you in some future article or book I write. Please check one of the boxes below and I will honor your wishes in that regard.

☐   Yes, you may quote from the following comments.

_____

(Name, please print)

☐   No, I prefer that you do not quote me.

_____

(Signature)

Thank you for responding to this request. Your time and thoughts are much appreciated. Please feel free to contact me if you have and questions or further comments.

Sincerely,

_____

(Your name, address, and e-mail)

Resource G

Selected Bibliography

Bienvenu, S. (1999). *The presentation skills workshop: Helping people create and deliver great presentations* (The Trainer's Workshop Series). Baltimore, MD: Department of Health and Mental Hygiene.

Bloom, P. J. (2000). *Workshop essentials: Planning and presenting dynamic workshops.* Seattle, WA: New Horizons.

Boylan, B. (2001). *What's your point? The 3-step method for making effective presentations.* Avon, MA: Adams Media.

Bredeson, P. V. (2002). *Designs for learning: A new architecture for professional development in schools.* Thousand Oaks, CA: Corwin.

Brewer, E. W. (1997). *13 proven ways to get your message across: The essential reference for teachers, trainers, presenters, and speakers.* Thousand Oaks, CA: Corwin.

Brody, M., & Kent, S. (1992). *Power presentations: How to connect with your audience and sell your ideas.* New York: John Wiley.

Caffarella, R. S. (2001). *Planning programs for adult learners: A practical guide for educators, trainers, and staff developers* (2nd ed.). San Francisco: Jossey-Bass.

Clark, D. (2005). *Training and development manual.* Retrieved May 14, 2005, from http://www.nwlink.com/~donclark/hrd.html

Costa, A. L., & Garmston, R. J. (2002). *Cognitive coaching: A foundation for renaissance schools* (2nd ed.). Norwood, MA: Christopher-Gordon.

Diresta, D. (1998). *Knockout presentations: How to deliver your message with power, punch, and pizzazz.* Madison, WI: Chandler House Press.

Finkelstein, E. (2002). *How to do everything with PowerPoint®.* New York: McGraw-Hill Osborne Media.

Franklin, E. (2002). *Relax your neck, liberate your shoulders: The ultimate exercise program for tension relief.* Heightstown, NJ: Princeton Book Company.

Garmston, R. (2005). *The presenter's fieldbook: A practical guide* (2nd ed.). Norwood, MA: Christopher-Gordon.

James, T., & Shephard, D. (2001). *Presenting magically: Transforming your stage presence with NLP.* Norwalk, CT: Crown House.

Jolles, R. L. (2000). *How to run seminars and workshops: Presentation skills for consultants, trainers, and teachers* (2nd ed.). New York: John Wiley.

Klatt, B. (1999). *The ultimate training workshop handbook: A comprehensive guide to leading successful workshops and training programs.* New York: McGraw-Hill.

Loucks-Horsley, S., Love, N., Stiles, K. E., Mundry, S. & Hewson, P. W. (2003). *Designing professional development for teachers of science and mathematics* (2nd ed.). Thousand Oaks, CA: Corwin.

McConnon, S. (2005). *Presenting with power: Captivate, motivate, inspire, persuade.* How to Books.

Mundry, S., Britton, E., Raizen, S. A., & Loucks-Horsley, S. (2000). *Designing successful professional meetings and conferences in education: Planning, implementation, and evaluation.* Thousand Oaks, CA: Corwin.

Newstrom, J. W., & Scannell, E. E. (1997). *The big book of presentation games: Wake-em-up tricks, icebreakers, and other fun stuff.* New York: McGraw-Hill.

Peoples, D. A. (1992). *Presentations plus: David Peoples' proven techniques* (Rev. ed.). New York: John Wiley.

Sarnoff, D. (1983). *Make the most of your best: A complete program for presenting yourself and your ideas with confidence and authority* (1st Owl Book ed.). New York: Henry Holt.

Shenson, H. L. (1990). *How to develop and promote successful seminars and workshops: The definitive guide to creating and marketing seminars, workshops, classes, and conferences.* New York: John Wiley.

Shephard, K. (2005). *Presenting at conferences, seminars and meetings.* Thousand Oaks, CA: Sage.

Sutton, H. (1997). *Speaking without fear or nervousness* (audiotape). Careertrack.

References

Allen, R. (2005). *5-day brain compatible facilitator training: Presenting with the brain in mind* (p. 53). San Diego, CA: The Brain Store.

Brookfield, S. D. (1993). Understanding consulting as an adult education process. In L. J. Zachary & S. Vernon (Eds.), *The adult educator as consultant* (New Directions for Adult and Continuing Education, No. 58, pp. 5–13). San Francisco, CA: Jossey-Bass.

Clance, P. (1985). *The impostor phenomenon.* Atlanta, GA: Peachtree.

Clarke, B. A., & Clarke, D. M. (1996). Enjoyable and worthwhile inservice presentations: We'd like to see that! *Prime Number, 11*(1), 19–21.

Díaz-Maggioli, G. (2004). Professional development today. *Teacher-centered professional development* (Chapter 1). Alexandria, VA: Association for Supervision and Curriculum Development (ASCD).

Eller, J. (2004). *Effective group facilitation in education.* Thousand Oaks, CA: Corwin.

Gardner, H. (1983). *Frames of mind: The theory of multiple intelligences.* New York: Basic Books.

Gardner, H. (1999). *Intelligence reframed: Multiple intelligences for the 21st century.* New York: Basic Books.

Hunter, M. (1982). *Mastery teaching.* El Sequndo, CA: TIP Publications.

Hunter, R. (2004). *Madeline Hunter's mastery teaching: Increasing instructional effectiveness in elementary and secondary schools.* Thousand Oaks, CA: Corwin.

Jensen, E. (1998). *Trainer's bonanza.* San Diego, CA: The Brain Store.

Kaagan, S. S. (2004). *30 reflective staff development exercises for educators.* Thousand Oaks, CA: Corwin.

National Staff Development Council. (2004). *Supporting school-based staff developers.* Retrieved May 20, 2005, from http://www.nsdc.org/connect/projects/schoolbased.cfm

Showers, B., Joyce, B., & Bennett, B. (1987). Synthesis of research on staff development: A framework for future study and a state-of-the-art analysis. *Educational Leadership, 45*(3), 77–87.

Steffy, B., Wolfe, M., Pasch, S., & Enz, B. (2000). *Life cycle of the career teacher.* Thousand Oaks, CA: Corwin.

Viens, J., & Kallenbach, S. (2004). *Multiple intelligences and adult literacy: A sourcebook for practitioners.* New York: Teachers College Press.

Villani, S. (2005). Mentoring promotes teacher leadership. In H. Portner (Ed.), *Mentoring promotes teacher leadership* (pp. 169–211). Thousand Oaks, CA: Corwin.

Zemke, R., & Zemke, S. (1984, March 9). 30 things we know for sure about adult learning. *Innovation Abstracts, 6*(8). Retrieved February 10, 2005, from <http://www.cccu.org/resourcecenter/resID.2207, parentCatID.263/rc_detail.asp>

Index

**CORWIN
PRESS**

The Corwin Press logo—a raven striding across an open book—represents the union of courage and learning. Corwin Press is committed to improving education for all learners by publishing books and other professional development resources for those serving the field of PreK–12 education. By providing practical, hands-on materials, Corwin Press continues to carry out the promise of its motto: **"Helping Educators Do Their Work Better."**